A Message to Parents

Every family has its own story.

Some are built by biology, others by choice, circumstance, or incredible journeys of hope and love.

LUMA, THE GREAT FOREST AND MIRROR OF LOVE was written to gently celebrate this beautiful truth, that families come in many shapes and sizes, and what matters most is the love that holds them together.

For children who come from unique beginnings, like surrogacy, adoption, solo parenting, or chosen families, this story offers a gentle mirror of belonging. For all children, it's an invitation to embrace difference, grow empathy, and understand that no two families look exactly the same and that's a wonderful thing.

May this story help open hearts, spark meaningful conversations, and remind every reader, big or small, that being different is not something to question, it's something to celebrate.

With love,
Paul

This is Luma
Luma is small
Luma is pink, fuzzy and sparkles in the sunlight.

But sometimes Luma feels a little different.

While Luma's friends have families who all look the same as each other, Luma's family was formed in a special way, Luma was a gift, a very special gift, given to her parents so they could raise her with all the love in their hearts.

Luma knows she is loved, but sometimes she wonders "why doesn't my family look like everyone else's?"

Not far from where Luma lives is a big, beautiful forest full of wiggly streams, glowing bugs, and trees so tall they tickle the clouds.

Some say a magical mirror is hidden deep inside this forest. And this mirror? It shows you something important, something only you can see.

So one sunny morning, filled with a curious heart and a little bit of hope, Luma decided to set off on an adventure to see if she could find it.

As Luma walked under the tall trees, she heard the sounds of chirping. High up in the branches was a family of birds. Luma decided to climb up to say hello. As she did, she noticed something interesting…some of the little birds looked different! Some were fluffy, some had spots and one had extra long feathers.

"Not all of us hatched from the same egg" explained one of the parent birds. "We found each other and we're a family because we love each other."

Luma smiled. That felt…familiar.

Luma kept walking deeper into the great forest, where she came across a shallow quiet pond. Turtles were sunbathing on warm stones, big ones, tiny ones, blue shells, green shells, even some with spots!

"We're a patchwork family" said one turtle smiling. "Some of us were adopted, some were raised by aunties and grandparents, but we are all family just the same."

Luma's heart felt a little lighter. But her legs were getting tired, "what if I never find the magical mirror?" she wondered.

Soon, the trail split...left? or right? Luma didn't know which way to go.

Suddenly, a family of glowing foxes danced out from behind a bush, their tails sparkling as bright as stars.

Luma followed them down the path. As they walked, Luma told them all about how her family was different. The foxes nodded along.

"Families come in all shapes" said one. "Some have two parents, some have one, and some have a whole bunch! It's love that holds us all together. That's what makes a family."

As she approached the very heart of the forest, Luma saw something shiny between the trees. "Wow" she whispered, "could it be?"

Luma stepped closer. There it was! The magical mirror, it stood tall among the glowing mushrooms and rustling leaves. But it wasn't golden like the stories had said.

It glowed soft pink, just like her. Taking a deep breath, Luma stepped closer and the mirror began to change.

But the mirror didn't show Luma just one reflection, instead it shifted, showing all the different families Luma had met along the way.

Luma saw the bird family in the nest, all different but full of love, the patchwork turtles sunbathing together, the glow tail foxes dancing in the trees, and then, finally, Luma saw her own family. Smiling, loving, proud.

Words then slowly appeared on the mirror:

"Families come in many shapes and sizes and are made in many different ways, but all are built with love. You are exactly where you are meant to be."

Luma's heart felt warm and full. She didn't feel different in a sad way anymore.

She felt special. She felt seen. She felt loved.

Families Come in Many
Shapes And Sizes,
And Are Made in
Many Different Ways.
But All Are Built
With Love.

You Are Exactly Where
You Are Meant To Be.

With a big, happy smile, Luma turned to head home, ready to tell her family everything about her adventure to the great forest!

www.ingramcontent.com/pod-product-compliance
Lightning Source LLC
LaVergne TN
LVHW070613080526
838200LV00103B/351